Firefighters Help Us

Greg Roza

ROSEN COMMON CORE READERS

Rosen Classroom™

New York

Published in 2013 by The Rosen Publishing Group, Inc.
29 East 21st Street, New York, NY 10010

Book Design: Michael Harmon

Photo Credits: Cover Ronald Caswell/Shutterstock.com; p. 5 Monkey Business Images/Shutterstock.com; p. 7 Jerry Sharp/Shutterstock.com; p. 9 EGD/Shutterstock.com; p. 11 (firefighter) Lilac Mountain/Shutterstock.com; p. 11 (fire) Dale A Stork/Shutterstock.com; p. 13 EGD/Shutterstock.com; p. 15 Jag_cs/Shutterstock.com; p. 16 (plane) ftwitty/Shutterstock.com.

ISBN: 978-1-4488-8701-9
6-pack ISBN: 978-1-4488-8702-6

Manufactured in the United States of America

CPSIA Compliance Information: Batch #WS12RC: For further information contact Rosen Publishing, New York, New York at 1-800-237-9932.

Word Count: 33

Contents

Firefighters do a lot for us.

CAPTAIN
FD
FIREFIGHTER

Firefighters put out fires with water.

TOWER 49 LADDER
CHARDON FIRE DEPARTMENT
CHARDON

Firefighters save people from fires.

LOS ANGELES
COUNTY
FIRE DEPT.
EMT

Firefighters save animals from fires.

WSFPD
FIRE-RESCUE
39
FIREFIGHTER

Firefighters help people who are hurt.

LOS ANGEL
FIRE DEPARTM
PARAMEDIC
1806
LOS ANGELES CITY
FIRE
DEPARTMENT
LAFD

Some firefighters jump from planes!

Words to Know

fire

firefighters

plane

Index